Amelia Glazner is an independent actress known in South Texas for her roles in various short films, including *The Art of Dying*, an official selection of the RockPort Film Festival 2022. *We're All Healing Here*—a feat of practical wisdom—is her debut publication and marks her entrance into the literary world. When she's not acting or writing, Amelia can be found immersed in nature photography, reading, or vlogging on her YouTube channel, *UniquelyAmelia*. You can also find her on Instagram: *@uniquelyamelia.*

Amelia Glazner

We're All Healing Here

AUSTIN MACAULEY PUBLISHERS®

LONDON • CAMBRIDGE • NEW YORK • SHARJAH

Ordering Information
Quantity sales: Special discounts are available on quantity purchases by corporations, associations, and others. For details, contact the publisher at the address below.

Publisher's Cataloging-in-Publication data
Glazner, Amelia
We're All Healing Here

ISBN 9798895432907 (Paperback)
ISBN 9798895432914 (ePub e-book)

Library of Congress Control Number: 2025905669

www.austinmacauley.com/us

First Published 2025
Austin Macauley Publishers LLC
40 Wall Street, 33rd Floor, Suite 3302
New York, NY 10005
USA

mail-usa@austinmacauley.com
+1 (646) 5125767

Thank you to everyone who encouraged me to write this and share my words with the world. I've been writing for so long but never had the courage to put myself out there—until now.

A special thanks to my brother, Joshua Glazner, for always believing in me and encouraging me to keep going when times were tough. Another heartfelt thank you to my mom, Andrea Doucette, for being my role model and safe space during the hardest moments.

Now, I want to dedicate a BIG thank you to my best friend, Jonah. He has always supported me and saw my potential long before I ever did. He never let a day go by without reminding me of how capable I am. I'll never be able to fully repay him for the love and encouragement he's shown me throughout this journey—it means more to me than he'll ever know.

This book would not have been possible without the special people in my life. I love all of you and will continue to show my gratitude each and every day.

I also want to thank God for guiding me through every obstacle and allowing me to turn my experiences into art.

And finally, I want to thank *myself*—for never giving up and for pushing through everything that brought me to where I am today.

BROKEN

To heal, you first need to break…

1

In another universe
I know we are together
Running around
Holding hands
Loving each other like we want to in this one
But this isn't that universe

2

Are you happier without me?

3

How do you grieve someone who is still alive
To know they are still somewhere on this earth
But you can't have them...

4

Will you find me again?

5

I don't want to forget the sound of your voice
The taste of your lips
The feeling of your hand in mine
The sound of your laugh
The warmth of your embrace
Your hands on my waist
The smell of your clothes
The love that you showed
              but I made my choice

6

I wish you hated me

7

I'm sorry
I say to you after you hurt me
I'm sorry
I say to you yet again
I'm–
As time went on I began to realize
I wasn't apologizing to you; I was apologizing to myself

8

Our first hello was different from our last goodbye

9

My mind feels like a cage
Locked
No key in sight
Not even a lock on the door

10

You clipped my wings so I could no longer fly
Healing seeming impossible
Thinking to myself
Why even try

11

You told me to talk
You told me you'd listen
I opened up to you
God, I was a fool
For you to use it against me
Now you walk around with this knowledge
Who knows what version you tell
Coming from someone who used to know me so well

12

What happened to us
Where did it go wrong
How did you go from the one I imagined a life with
To someone I don't recognize at all

13

You feel comfortable in the uncomfortable
Never allowing yourself to experience true happiness

14

I'm here but am I *here*
Physically
I sit in this room
I drive this car
I am doing these things
But I am not *living* them

15

My mind spins
Like a spin cycle
One thought consumes me until I cannot breathe
Every outcome
Floods through my mind like a river
I am drowning

16

You get stuck in a loop from your past
Bringing your hurts into new relationships
Unknowingly comparing, pulling away
Never knowing if it's real or if it's for show
Can I ever trust again
Will I ever trust again

17

I do not recognize the person staring back at me in this
mirror
Those aren't my eyes
That isn't my faded smile
I don't recognize myself anymore

18

Why can't I see myself like they do
What is so different about my perception
Where everyone sees "perfection"
I see rejection

19

My heart yearns for you
Your touch
Your taste
Your presence
Your love
You
My heart aches for you

20

I don't remember what I look like anymore
I see this person in the mirror
But where am I

21

You love me
Oh… I couldn't tell
You're sorry
Oh… if only I didn't know you so well
There are only so many times you can tell me these things
because they start to sound exactly like that
Things

22

Your love was like a drug
I used to think that was a good thing until it wasn't
You withheld your love from me until I broke
To shower me with it, to give me my fix
You knew exactly how to keep me
When I was so close to letting you go
You gave me another fix
Your love was like a drug and I couldn't get enough

23

I felt like your toy
You kept me in your drawer and took me out when you
needed me
Blinded by the love I thought you had
You didn't love me; you loved what I had
And I let you do it

24

I pour it all out for it to be taken away from me
I try again just for it to be stripped away
I try once more believing you can replenish it
To be fooled yet again
There are only so many times I can try until I have nothing
left to give

25

Please don't leave me; I don't want you to go
Please don't leave me; I can't do this without you
Please don't leave me; I can be better
Please don't leave me; I–
Please–

Why do I have to beg for you to stay

HEALING

Healing doesn't turn you back into who you once were

26

When I think of you
I smile
Funny even though we haven't spoken in a while
All the good memories we shared
I felt you truly cared
So instead of tears
I'm filled with cheer
Even now when we've ended
I'm learning to live with a heart unamended

27

There is no "wrong person"
There is only timing
You can love someone and grow apart
That is the part of healing you have to understand

28

Your words replay in my head
And every day ahead
I'll continue to make you proud
Even when you aren't around

29

You can love and grow apart
You can love and last forever

30

We weren't always bad
There was a time we were perfect for each other
We were both imperfect people with pain
Not trying to take it out on each other
But in the end, we did
Words that we spoke, and things left unsaid
We needed each other for a time
And now that time has passed
We do not need each other anymore
But I will always be grateful for the time we had
Because we truly weren't always bad

31

At one point in my life, I believed you were the one
We were perfectly imperfect together
Two souls entangled as one
But that was one point
This is now
We are no longer one
We are two
Very far from where we used to be
But even though we are apart now
I know we were in each other's lives for a reason
And for that I am grateful

32

A new place
New faces
A change of pace
Won't truly heal you
It is merely a mask
The view may change but the trauma will remain the same
To truly heal, you need to look within

33

You set unrealistic goals for yourself
Then let yourself down
Ultimately giving up
Give yourself grace
Give yourself patience
Just as the hurt developed over time
The healing with also take place over time

34

My mind is like a cage
Locked
But there is a key in sight
The lock is now visible to me

35

You clipped my wings, but they can grow back
Healing is in my reach
Thinking to myself,
it's time to get on the right track

36

You can *heal* without a time limit
You can *help* without being pushed around
You can *love* without being taken advantage of
You can have *peace* without sacrificing your sanity

37

Healing is uncomfortable
Healing is hurting
Healing is taking a leap
If it was easy it wouldn't be worth achieving

38

A big part of healing that you have to understand is
It's not always what you want
You can't control everything
That person
That place
That experience
That thing you want so badly to keep
It might not be a part of your next step
And you must learn to be ok with that
If you truly want to heal

39

Do not let your old mindset determine your new one

40

I am starting to recognize that person in the mirror
Those eyes seem a little brighter
The lines from my smile are less faded
I am starting to recognize myself again

41

You can't expect to be who you once were when you heal
You are a different person now
Embrace it
The change is who you are now
And that is okay

42

Once you learn that healing takes time
You can give yourself the space to do so

43

Even flowers need time to bloom

44

Dwell on the past and you'll never escape
Focus on the present and you'll truly live
Worry about the future and you'll never grow

45

You can wish something never happened
You can wish you could change the past
But worrying about it and wishing won't fix anything
The only way out is through
You need to look forward and instead of wishing
Work to make sure that doesn't happen again
Work to define your future
The past is the past
The now is the now
The future is tomorrow.

46

Falling back into patterns
Doesn't mean you've failed
What matters now is
Where you go from there

47

To get perspective you have to be willing to hear someone else's perspective

48

You are worthy of love
You are worthy of healing
You don't need to let your past determine your newfound
feelings

49

You didn't deserve what you allowed yourself to go through

50

Just as the sun set and arose the next day
So will you.

LØVE(D)

We allow ourselves the love we believe we deserve

51

When all hope felt gone
The feeling of being alone for so long
A light shined from you to me
Showing me I can be loved the way I always dreamt I'd be

52

My heart was broken over and over again
And you are here picking up all the pieces
Fixing a heart you didn't even break
And I would go through it all again
If it meant it would lead me to you

53

To love another person you have to remember
It won't always be perfect
You are going to fight
You are going to disagree
But love is how you react to these situations
And how you come out the other side
Together

54

Maturing is realizing
You aren't supposed to be fighting each other
You are supposed to fight the problem
Together

55

True love is determined after a fight
How did they react
How did they respond to you
How did you react
How did you respond to them
Love even when times get hard

56

Your love is a poem written in my heart

57

The light fills the room when your name pops up on my
screen
My cheeks begin to hurt from the smile stuck upon me
I wonder how you make me feel this way
How you make someone so afraid to fall again, dive
headfirst into love with you

58

Allow yourself to be loved the right way
You deserve it

59

My mind is an open door
Unlocked
I found the key
The lock is now open
I am free

60

You clipped my wings, but I can fly once again
Healing became healed
Thinking to myself, *It was never "if" but "when"*

61

You cannot rely on others to determine your own worth
Words feel nice in the moment
But your true perception of yourself lasts a lifetime

62

I woke up again today
I got out of bed but left the comforter a mess
But I got up today
I went into the kitchen and ate today, not much
But I ate today
I took a shower and got ready, with no makeup
But I got ready today
I got through the day, that's it
I got through it
And that's enough

63

Love yourself more than anyone else could

64

Think of the person you love the most
How would you show them
How would you celebrate them
How would you take care of them
Now do that for yourself

65

I recognize that person in the mirror – it's me!
Those are my eyes!
That smile is my smile!
I recognize myself and I love her

66

Love yourself like you would love your favorite person

67

Focus on the present so the future you doesn't look back on
this moment and wish it were different
The past is the past
The present is now
The future is tomorrow

68

I'd look for you in every universe
I believe we have a story in them all
Because,
The love I feel for you
Is strong enough for me to be sure
That you're the one I love in every single one of them

69

Billions of people on earth
Thousands of years to have lived
Yet, here we are
Blessed to be together
To have found one another
And I'll always be grateful for that
I'll always be grateful for you

70

The world used to be so loud
The constant rush of endless thoughts
I would cover myself in the darkness until they passed
But,
Ever since you
The world has gotten quiet
And those endless thoughts
Don't seem so inevitable anymore

71

Foggy eyes turned clear
A clouded mind greeted by the sun
Trauma became lessons
And I am grateful for every single one

72

I used to believe the kind of love I strived for wasn't real
It was only a myth
To now realize it's just the opposite
It does exist and it is oh-so-real
If I am capable of giving the love I strive for
Then so is someone else

73

Don't allow the loss of a love you once had to change your perception of the love you will gain from it

74

Forgiveness is the key to love
That hurt
That pain
That you hold onto
Won't change the past or fix the present
You need to forgive and love like you would want someone
to do for you

75

Your current situation is not your final destination
Remember where you once were and where you are now
You have come so far.
Remember your strength and your determination
You can and will do hard things
You are worthy of a happy and healthy life
We're all healing here